THE DATA-DRIVEN DRIVEN CLASSROOM

How do I use student data to improve my instruction?

CRAIG A.
MERTLER

 Alexandria, VA USA

Website: www.ascd.org
E-mail: books@ascd.org

www.ascdarias.org

Printed in the United States of America. Cover art © 2014 by ASCD. ASCD publications present a variety of viewpoints. The views expressed or implied in this book should not be interpreted as official positions of the Association.

ASCD LEARN TEACH LEAD® and ASCD ARIAS™ are trademarks owned by ASCD and may not be used without permission. All other referenced trademarks are the property of their respective owners.

PAPERBACK ISBN: 978-1-4166-1975-8   ASCD product #SF114082
Also available as an e-book (see Books in Print for the ISBNs).

Library of Congress Cataloging-in-Publication Data

Mertler, Craig A.
  The data-driven classroom : how do I use student data to improve my instruction? / Craig A. Mertler.
     pages cm. — (ASCD ARIAS)
  Includes bibliographical references.
  ISBN 978-1-4166-1975-8 (pbk. : alk. paper) 1. Educational tests and measurements. 2. Effective teaching. I. Title.
  LB3051.M4655 2014
  371.26—dc23
                                                                    2014021970

21 20 19 18 17 16 15 14   1 2 3 4 5 6 7 8 9 10

THE DATA-DRIVEN CLASSROOM

How do I use student data to improve my instruction?

Want to earn a free ASCD Arias e-book?
Your opinion counts! Please take 2–3 minutes to give
us your feedback on this publication. All survey
respondents will be entered into a drawing to
win an ASCD Arias e-book.

Please visit
www.ascd.org/ariasfeedback

Thank you!

Introduction to Data-Driven Educational Decision Making

Teachers have been using data about students to inform their instructional decision making since the early movement to formalize education in the United States. Good teachers tend to use numerous types of data and gather them from a wide variety of sources. Historically speaking, however, teachers have typically not incorporated data resulting from the administration of standardized tests (Mertler & Zachel, 2006).

In recent years—beginning with the adequate yearly progress requirements of No Child Left Behind (NCLB) and continuing with Race to the Top (RTTT) and the Common Core State Standards (CCSS) assessments—using standardized test data has become an accountability requirement. With each passing year, there seems to be an increasing level of accountability placed on school districts, administrators, and teachers. Compliance with the requirements inherent in NCLB, RTTT, and the CCSS has become a focal point for schools and districts. For example, most states now annually rate or "grade" the effectiveness of their respective school districts on numerous (approximately 25–35) performance indicators, the vast majority of which are based on student performance on standardized tests.

As a result, the notion of data-driven decision making has steadily gained credence, and it has become crucial for classroom teachers and building-level administrators to understand how to make data-driven educational decisions.

Data-driven educational decision making refers to the process by which educators examine assessment data to identify student strengths and deficiencies and apply those findings to their practice. This process of critically examining curriculum and instructional practices relative to students' actual performance on standardized tests and other assessments yields data that help teachers make more accurately informed instructional decisions (Mertler, 2007; Mertler & Zachel, 2006). Local assessments—including summative assessments (classroom tests and quizzes, performance-based assessments, portfolios) and formative assessments (homework, teacher observations, student responses and reflections)—are also legitimate and viable sources of student data for this process.

The "Old Tools" Versus the "New Tools"

The concept of using assessment information to make decisions about instructional practices and intervention strategies is nothing new; educators have been doing it forever. It is an integral part of being an effective educational professional. In the past, however, the *sources* of that assessment information were different; instructional decisions were more often based on what I refer to as the "old tools" of the professional educator: intuition, teaching philosophy, and personal experience. These are all valid sources of information and, taken together, constitute a sort of holistic "gut instinct" that has long helped guide educators' instruction. This gut instinct should not be ignored. However, it shouldn't be teachers' *only* compass when it comes to instructional decision making.

The problem with relying solely on the old tools as the basis for instructional decision making is that they do not add up to a systematic process (Mertler, 2009). For example, as educators, we often like to try out different instructional approaches and see what works. Sounds simple enough, but the trial-and-error process of choosing a strategy, applying it in the classroom, and judging how well it worked is different for every teacher. How do we decide which strategy to try, and how do we know whether it "worked"? The process is not very efficient or consistent and can lead to ambiguous results (and sometimes a good deal of frustration).

Trial and error does have a place in the classroom: through our various efforts and mistakes, we learn what *not* to do, what did *not* work. Even when our great-looking ideas fail in practice, we have not failed. In fact, this process is beneficial to the teaching and learning process. There is nothing wrong with trying out new ideas in the classroom. It's just that this cannot be our only way to develop strong instructional strategies.

I firmly believe that teaching can be an art form: there are some skills that just cannot be taught. I am sure that if you think back to your own education, you can recall a teacher who just "got" you. When you walked out of that teacher's classroom, you felt inspired. Conversely, we've all had teachers who were on the opposite end of that "effectiveness spectrum"—who just did *not* get it, who were not artists in their classrooms. Even young students are able to sense that.

The concept of teaching as an art form is an important and integral part of the educational process, and I don't intend to diminish it. Rather, what I want to do is expand on it by integrating some additional ideas and strategies that build on this notion of good classroom teaching. The old tools do not seem to be enough anymore (LaFee, 2002); we must balance them with the "new tools" of the professional educator. These new tools, which consist mainly of standardized test and other assessment results, provide an additional source of information upon which teachers can base curricular and instructional decisions. This data-driven component facilitates a more scientific and systematic approach to the decision-making process. If we think of the old tools as the "art" of teaching, then the new tools are the "science" of teaching.

I do not think that the art of teaching and the science of teaching are mutually exclusive. Ideally, educators would practice both. In this publication, however, I focus on the *data-driven science of teaching.*

A Systematic Approach

Taking the data-driven approach to instructional decision making requires us to consider alternative instructional and assessment strategies in a systematic way. When we teach our students the scientific method, they learn to generate ideas, develop hypotheses, design a scientific investigation, collect data, analyze those data, draw conclusions, and then start the cycle all over again by developing new hypotheses. Likewise, educational practitioners can use the scientific method to explore and weigh our own options related to teaching and learning. This process is still trial and error, but the "trial" piece becomes a lot more systematic and incorporates a good deal of professional reflection (Mertler, 2009). And, like the scientific method, the decision-making process I describe in the following sections is *cyclical*: the data teachers gather through the process are continually used to inform subsequent instruction. The process doesn't just end with the teacher either deciding the strategy is a winner or shrugging and moving on to a new strategy that he or she hopes will work better.

A major reason teachers don't rely more on assessment data to make instructional decisions is the sheer volume of information provided on standardized test reports. One teacher comment I often hear is, "There is so much information here that I don't even know where to start!" One way to make the process less overwhelming is to focus your attention on a few key pieces of information from test reports and other assessment results and essentially ignore other data, which are often duplicative.

Another anecdotal comment I often hear from teachers provides a reason why many educators resist relying on assessment data—that is, the belief that using test results to guide classroom decision making reduces the educational process to a businesslike transaction. It's true that in business settings, data are absolutely essential. Information about customers, inventory, and sales, for example, are crucial in determining a business's success or failure. In contrast, in education we tend to focus more on the "human" side of things. Rightfully so, of course: kids are living, breathing entities, whereas data are abstract. For many educators, this truly makes *data* a four-letter word (LaFee, 2002). Yet we don't need to view data as antithetical to the educational process; there's room for the data side *and* the human side.

The idea of data-driven decision making is not new, but incorporating data into instruction does take some practice on the part of the classroom teacher. The following section should shed some light on this practice and help make it a less intimidating process.

Understanding How to Look at the Data: Advice and Caveats

Educators can effectively use student assessment data to guide the development of either individualized intervention strategies or large-group instructional revisions. Regardless of the purpose and goals of the decision-making process, it is important to heed some cautionary advice before examining the results of standardized tests.

Generally speaking, standardized achievement tests are intended to survey basic knowledge or skills across a broad domain of content (Chase, 1999). A standardized test may contain as many as seven or eight subtests in subjects such as mathematics, reading, science, and social studies. Each subtest is then further broken down to assess specific skills or knowledge within its content area. For example, the reading subtest may include subsections for vocabulary, reading comprehension, synonyms, antonyms, word analogies, and word origins. One of these particular subsections may contain only five or six actual test items. Therefore, it is essential to interpret student performance on any given subtest or subsection with a great deal of care.

Specifically, educators must be aware of the potential for careless errors or lucky guesses to skew a student's score in a particular area, especially if the scores are reported as percentile ranks or if the number of items answered correctly is used to classify student performance according to such labels as "below average," "average," and "above average." This caveat also applies to local classroom assessments, including larger unit tests, final exams, or comprehensive projects. Whatever the type of assessment, it is important to avoid *over-interpretation*—that is, making sweeping, important decisions about students or instruction on the basis of limited sets of data (Russell & Airasian, 2012). Although over-interpreting results does not *guarantee* erroneous decision making, it is certainly more likely to result in flawed, inaccurate, or less-valid instructional decisions.

Prior to making any significant instructional or curricular decisions, it is therefore crucial to examine not only the raw scores, percentile ranks, and the like but also the *total number of items* on a given test, subtest, or subsection (Mertler, 2003, 2007). In addition, educators should consult and factor in multiple sources and types of student data to get a more complete view of student progress or achievement. These additional sources of data may be formal (e.g., chapter tests, class projects, or performance assessments) or informal (e.g., class discussions, homework assignments, or formative assessments). Looking at a broader array of data can help teachers avoid putting too much weight on a single measure of student performance and, therefore, reduce the risk of making inaccurate and invalid decisions about student learning and teaching effectiveness.

In the following sections, we will look at the two main ways classroom teachers can use student assessment results as part of the data-driven decision-making process: (1) developing specific intervention strategies for individual students, and (2) revising instruction for entire classes or courses (Mertler, 2002, 2003).

Decision Making for Individual Interventions

Figure 1 depicts the process for examining assessment results to make instructional decisions and develop intervention strategies for *individual* students (Mertler, 2007).

The steps shown in Figure 1 constitute a "universal" process for using standardized test data and other assessment results to guide intervention decisions. The process is universal in that *it can be applied to any situation, regardless of grade level, subject area, type of instruction, or types of skills being taught.* Seen separately, these steps are not

FIGURE 1: **Universal Process for Identifying Areas for Individual Intervention**

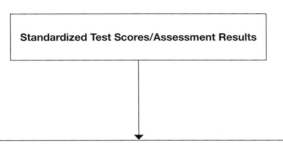

Standardized Test Scores/Assessment Results

1. Identify any content, skill, or subtest areas where the student performed below average.

2. Rank the content or skill areas in order of poorest performance.

3. From this list, select 1–2 content areas to serve as the focus of the intervention.

4. Identify new or different methods of instruction, reinforcement, assessment, and so on to meet the needs of the individual student.

Development of Intervention

particularly complex, but taken together they represent an ongoing, systematic process that enables educators to

- Take a large amount of assessment data.
- Narrow the focus for potential interventions on the subtests, content areas, or skills where student performance was weakest.
- Further pare down that list by focusing on the one or two most critical content or skill areas.
- Develop an intervention strategy for addressing the particular weakness(es) by identifying different modes of instruction, reinforcement or practice, or methods of assessing student learning and mastery.

Typically, a teacher might know which students in his or her class are struggling (by means of assessment performance or simple observations) but likely would not know the *specific* areas or skills where interventions should be targeted. The process begins with the teacher examining test reports or other obtained assessment results and identifying any content, skill, or subtest areas where a given student performed poorly or below average. If the teacher identifies more than one problem area, he or she should rank those areas in order of perceived severity of deficiency. The one or two highest-priority areas should then be selected as the focus of the intervention. Finally, the teacher should identify, develop, and implement new or different methods of instruction, reinforcement, or assessment to meet the needs of the individual student (Mertler, 2007).

An example of student-level decision making follows.

Example #1: Student-Level Decision Making

On the whole, Mrs. Garcia's 1st grade class had been doing quite well in all tested areas of reading (phonemic awareness, alphabetic principle, vocabulary, and fluency and comprehension) on both the benchmark assessments and the monitoring assessments of the district-adopted standardized reading test. One student, however, was struggling with certain aspects of the assessments. Jacob seemed to be strong in phonemic awareness, having surpassed the target in the October benchmark assessment, and he met the target score for alphabetic principle in December. However, he was having trouble in the area of oral reading fluency. He scored slightly below the target in October and did not show any improvement in the December assessment, although the target goal had increased. Essentially, the assessments indicated that Jacob was regressing in oral reading fluency.

Mrs. Garcia knew that Jacob needed some individualized support to progress toward the grade-appropriate goals. She decided to implement weekly oral reading fluency interventions. The purpose of these intervention activities was to provide continual reinforcement of fluent reading skills. In addition, she decided to check Jacob's ability to recognize sight words to see if he might also need remediation in that area. If this was the case, Mrs. Garcia knew that helping him improve his sight word recognition would also increase his oral fluency.

How to Know Whether Your Interventions Have Been Effective

As you may have guessed, the key to determining the effectiveness of your intervention strategies is to collect more data. In essence, determining intervention effectiveness is a continuation of the process depicted in Figure 1. This is a *cyclical process*: teachers collect and analyze data to inform their initial intervention attempts; collect data after implementation to determine the effectiveness of the intervention; and then collect even more data to continually assess the intervention's overall effectiveness in terms of student learning. In between data collection points, teachers continue to use assessment data to adjust or revise the intervention strategy. Note that the cyclical nature of this process means it is potentially never-ending. It is important not to see the process as just another item to check off your to-do list. Instead, this ongoing process of assessment of effectiveness and (potential) revision of the intervention should look like this:

→ Use of assessment data to determine initial intervention strategy → Implementation of intervention strategy → Collection of additional data on effectiveness of intervention strategy → Reassessment of effectiveness/revision of intervention strategy → [Repeat cycle as needed]

Continuation of Example #1: Assessment of Intervention Effectiveness

Mrs. Garcia firmly believed that routinely assessing and reinforcing Jacob's reading fluency and sight word recognition would help him progress toward grade-level goals. However, she knew that to support her belief, she needed to continually collect data to monitor Jacob's skills. Accordingly, each Thursday morning Mrs. Garcia administered an oral reading fluency monitoring assessment to Jacob. These were relatively brief reading assessments in which she asked Jacob to read aloud a passage consisting of five to seven sentences. In addition, she provided Jacob with a list of 10 age- and ability-appropriate words to see if he could recognize them by sight. Mrs. Garcia developed and printed a simple spreadsheet so that she could record the results of each of these two monitoring assessments every Thursday (see Figure 2).

After four weeks of implementing her intervention with Jacob, Mrs. Garcia began to notice a trend. His oral reading fluency began to improve, as indicated by the fact that he was making fewer errors each progressive week. She felt positive about Jacob's progress in this area, as well as her intervention. However, his sight word recognition, while improving slightly, was still quite a ways from the target goal. Based on these data, Mrs. Garcia felt that she should slightly revise her strategy for intervention with Jacob.

FIGURE 2: **Jacob's Weekly Assessment Chart**

Jacob Miller	Date					
	1/16	1/23	1/30	2/6	2/13	2/20
Oral Reading Fluency (errors)	7	7	4	3		
Sight Word Recognition (errors)	8/10	7/10	6/10	7/10		

She did not want to abandon the oral reading fluency reinforcement, for fear that he would regress, so she decided to continue working informally with Jacob on reading fluency each week but only assess him every other week. With respect to the sight word recognition, she decided to increase both reinforcement and assessment so that they occurred at the beginning and the end of each week. With this revised intervention, she could continue to support both areas where Jacob had demonstrated deficiencies while making sight word recognition the priority. Of course, Mrs. Garcia would continue to collect data in her spreadsheet to monitor Jacob's progress through the end of the school year.

Decision Making for Group-Level Instructional Revisions

When examining assessment results—whether from standardized tests or from local assessments (e.g., classroom tests or performance-based assessments)—for the purpose of revising instruction, the best practice is to interpret results provided for an entire class or course (Mertler, 2002; Mertler & Zachel, 2006). These results may be obtained from a class or group test report (available from the company responsible for scoring the test) or by conducting an informal item analysis of a local assessment. This information allows the classroom teacher to see how students are performing as a whole, across the curriculum. It is important to note that, in some situations—such as secondary school settings and perhaps even in some elementary settings—this process may be a collaborative one among teachers in which they teach the same subject matter and at the same grade level. This might happen as an informal collaboration or as a formal part of a professional learning community.

I want to reiterate here how important it is to avoid the pitfall of over-interpreting assessment data, regardless of the type of assessment administered. Over-interpreting too-small samples of data can lead to inaccurate conclusions, flawed decisions, and inappropriate and potentially ineffective instructional revisions. Again, before making instructional decisions, educators should take into account the total number of items on a given test, subtest, or subsection (Mertler, 2003, 2007).

An additional word of caution is in order. You are likely aware that most publishers of standardized achievement tests provide both criterion-referenced and norm-referenced results on individual student reports. Many criterion-referenced results are reported in terms of *average* performance (i.e., below average, average, and above average). It is important to remember that *average* simply means that half of the norm group scored above and half scored below that particular score.

Figure 3 depicts the process for examining assessment results to identify curricular or skill areas in which a large proportion of the student cohort (e.g., the class or grade level) is deficient and to make informed decisions about large-group instructional revisions. Like the process shown in Figure 1, this is a universal process that can be used in any situation, regardless of grade level, subject area, type of instruction, or types of skills being taught.

Adherence to the steps outlined in Figure 3 is crucial to getting a clear picture of any correlations between student performance and the curriculum or instructional practices (Mertler, 2007). The first step in this process is the identification of any content, skill, or subtest areas where high percentages of students performed below average (in the case of criterion-referenced test scores) or where group performance is low in relation to that of the norm group (in the case of norm-referenced test scores). Second, the teacher—or, perhaps, a collaborative group of teachers— ranks these identified areas of weakness in order of poorest student performance. The third step is to flag the top one or two problem areas for further examination: these will serve as the focus for any curricular or instructional revisions by the teacher(s). As part of this closer scrutiny, I strongly recommend that teachers consider addressing the following questions for these high-priority areas (note the high degree of professional reflection built into the questions):

FIGURE 3: **Universal Process for Identifying Areas for Large-Scale Instructional Revision**

Standardized Test Scores/Assessment Results

1. Identify any content, skill, or subtest areas where high percentages of students performed below average.

2. Based on these percentages, rank the content or skill areas in order of poorest performance.

3. From this list, select 1–2 areas to examine further by addressing the following questions:

- Where is this content addressed in our district's curriculum?
  - At what point in the school year is this content taught?
    - How are students taught this content?
  - How are students required to demonstrate that they have mastered this content?

4. Based on the answers to the questions above, identify new or different methods of instruction, reinforcement, assessment, and so on to meet the needs of the group.

Revised Instruction

- Where are these concepts/skills addressed in our district's curriculum?
- At what point in the school year are these concepts/ skills taught?
- How are students taught these concepts/skills?
- How are students required to demonstrate that they have mastered these concepts/skills? In other words, how are they assessed in the classroom?

Answers to these questions, as well as to others that will undoubtedly arise during the process, often provide important information that will ultimately guide decisions regarding instructional revisions. The specification of these revisions—which could consist of identifying new or different methods of instruction, incorporating new supplemental materials or activities, reorganizing the sequence of instructional topics, or developing or using different types of classroom assessments—constitutes the fourth and final step in the process.

An example of group-level decision making follows.

Example #2: Group-Level Decision Making

Mr. Scott is an 8th grade mathematics teacher. He was initially quite pleased as he looked over his class's score report from the most recent statewide mathematics achievement test. His class's average scaled score of 412 was well within the Proficient range, equal to the state average, and only slightly below that for the entire school and district. Only 21 percent of the students in his class achieved a score below the Proficient performance level—a lower percentage than the overall percentages in his school, in the district, and across the state. However, he knew that he needed to examine the results a little more closely: the fact that more than one-fifth of the total number of students in his classes had scored below the Proficient level indicated that there was room for improvement.

The mathematics test was broken down into five strands, and Mr. Scott's next step was to examine the results for each of them. His students' performance on the Measurement strand was good, with only 4 percent of the class scoring Below Proficient. He moved on to the Numbers, Number Sense, and Operations strand and found a different story: nearly one-third (30 percent) of his students scored Below Proficient on this strand. Although this performance concerned him, he wanted to examine the results for all strands and put them in appropriate context prior to making any decisions.

Over one-fourth (26 percent) of his class failed to meet the standard for Geometry and Spatial Sense, which was partially demonstrated in the results for released items. However, he was not quite as concerned as he might have been, since his class still outperformed students in the rest of the school, in the district, and across the state. He felt that this might be an area on which to focus some instructional revisions, but at this point, he wasn't sure it was the most critical area. Similarly, although there was room for improvement on the Patterns, Functions, and Algebra strand (with 16 percent scoring Below Proficient), Mr. Scott's students performed better than the comparison groups did. Again, he decided to hold off on making a decision about this strand.

The fifth strand, Data Analysis and Probability, worried Mr. Scott even before he looked at his students' results. Although he taught a unit on these very topics each year, the unit typically fell late in the year, just prior to (and sometimes just following) the administration of the statewide achievement tests. His students never seemed to do very well on this strand of the statewide achievement test, despite the fact that it was content he really enjoyed teaching and believed he taught well. He had sometimes thought that he might not be giving the students a fair chance to do well on this strand. Mr. Scott's review of the test results seemed to confirm this belief: students had difficulties with all three of the released items, and 22 percent scored below the Proficient level.

Although his class's performance on several strands indicated the need for some additional attention or instructional revisions, Mr. Scott ranked the five strands, in order of priority, as follows:

1. Data Analysis and Probability (22 percent Below Proficient).

2. Numbers, Number Sense, and Operations (30 percent Below Proficient).

3. Geometry and Spatial Sense (26 percent Below Proficient).

4. Patterns, Functions, and Algebra (16 percent Below Proficient).

5. Measurement (4 percent Below Proficient).

Notice that although Mr. Scott ranked numbers 2 through 5 according to the percentage of students who scored below the Proficient level, his highest-priority area was based not only on students' test results in the strand but also on how his students had historically responded to his teaching of the content. Based on his prioritization, he decided to make some changes to the Data Analysis and Probability unit. He decided to take a closer look at which concepts were most challenging for students and to move the unit up several weeks so that during the next school year, he would teach it as the first unit in the second semester of the school year. He reminded himself that he needed to be conscious that the shift would mean pushing back some other content later in the spring, closer to the administration of the test. He knew that his examination of next spring's test results would need to take into consideration this factor.

How to Know Whether Your Instructional Revisions Have Been Effective

Like the process for determining the effectiveness of individual student interventions, the process for determining the effectiveness of large-group instructional revisions should rely on the collection of additional data. Once again, these data are used in an ongoing cycle of assessing instructional effectiveness. The process should look like this:

→ Use of assessment data to prioritize areas for instructional revisions → Design and implementation of instructional revisions →

Collection of additional data on effectiveness of new instruction → Reassessment of effectiveness of instructional revisions → [Repeat cycle as needed]

The examination and assessment of the effectiveness of instructional revisions *must* be based on the collection of additional data; teachers should not rely exclusively on gut instinct to draw their conclusions and devise next steps. That said, teachers can and should use a variety of sources and types of data. Possible data include scores on formal assessments, such as unit tests, performance assessments, major class projects, collaborative group work, or district-wide, statewide, or national standardized tests. You may also find it beneficial to your individual decision-making process to include the results of informal assessments, such as homework or seatwork, teacher questions, class discussions, student or class journals, exit slips, one-minute papers, or "muddiest point" activities. In addition, teacher journals or other forms of your own professional reflection can serve as valuable sources of data.

Regardless of which additional sources of data you choose to incorporate, your ongoing data-driven decision-making process will be much better informed because of them. You can feel more confident in your findings when you are reviewing data from a variety of assessment types, perspectives, student activities, and even days and times.

Continuation of Example #2: Assessment of Instructional Revision Effectiveness

As the new school year began, Mr. Scott knew that he could not wait until the spring test was administered and scored to find out how well his instructional revision had worked. He recognized that those scores would likely be the most important indicator of his revision's effectiveness, but he wanted to do some things during the fall and winter to gauge from a more local perspective the extent to which his reorganization of content improved students' performance.

Mr. Scott decided to give this year's students a pre-test of sorts to determine their prior knowledge of mathematical concepts. Interestingly, the results of the pre-test were not that different from the results of last year's statewide math exam. He thought about trying to find ways to incorporate mini-lessons throughout the fall semester on all areas covered on the state exam. However, he knew that this approach could result in misleading information, since he was really only trying to target the Data Analysis and Probability strand. Instead, he decided to incorporate mini-lessons specifically focused on analysis and probability throughout the fall semester, leading up to the full unit. In addition, Mr. Scott asked his students to maintain journals, writing entries every two to three weeks about mathematical concepts they struggled with throughout the year. He provided them with class time to write these entries and collected and read their journals once a month.

Mr. Scott used data gleaned from the pre-test results and students' journals to inform his approach that first semester. His mini-lessons provided advanced introductions and, eventually, reinforcements related to data analysis and probability. He believed that this preliminary instruction would better prepare his students for the unit, which he began teaching in mid-January and completed one month later.

Following his administration of the unit test on data analysis and probability, Mr. Scott was happily surprised to see that his students had performed much better than he had anticipated, based on student performance the previous year. He believed that periodically introducing and reinforcing the concepts that had presented the most difficulty (according to both pre-test results and student journals) throughout the first half of the school year had provided students with a firm foundation to study this particular unit. He knew, however, that the final data on the effectiveness of his approach would be collected in two months, when the state exam was to be administered. He told himself that even if the student scores were not markedly better than the previous year's, he knew that they had a better understanding of the concepts in this strand.

When the results of the state mathematics exam arrived in May, Mr. Scott nervously reviewed the performance of his students. He was thrilled to see that the percentage of students below the Proficient level had decreased from 22 percent last year to 10 percent this year. Perhaps even more important was the fact that the percentages of students below the Proficient level in the remaining four strands held relatively constant. Mr. Scott knew that his instructional revisions had been effective, to a degree, but he also knew that he had much more work to do. He reviewed his students' performances in all five strands from this year's test and prioritized which of the strands he would target at the beginning of next year for introduction and reinforcement, to begin the next cycle of instructional improvements.

Action Planning for Future Instructional Cycles

Up to this point, we have examined processes for using student data to identify curricular or skill areas to target for revision and improvement. We have looked at these processes for both individual interventions and large-group instructional revisions. In addition, we have examined a secondary process for assessing the effectiveness of these interventions and revisions. We have established that all of these processes are cyclical in nature: although they may branch off into slightly different directions, they are essentially never-ending processes.

The challenge with this ongoing nature of data-driven decision making is that if your engagement in these processes progresses across multiple years, it will likely become increasingly difficult to keep track of where you have been and to map out where you might be headed. Therefore, some additional procedures for monitoring your progress and planning your future direction are warranted.

What Is Action Planning?

Action planning is an important part of these overall processes of data-driven decision making: it lays out a direction for the continuation of the decision-making process focused on student improvement while at the same time documenting current revisions and interventions. Action planning incorporates professional reflection, experience, and judgment into the process of sound educational decision making. When your data-driven processes span multiple school years—and, therefore, multiple students, courses, and even content areas—it can become increasingly difficult to maintain records of the various interventions and instructional revisions you have tried, including their rate of success and many other kinds of information you will undoubtedly want to remember at a later date.

Action planning consists of three components, including

1. Specifying and documenting current interventions or instructional revisions.

2. Maintaining evidence of the effectiveness of those interventions or revisions.

3. Planning ahead for the next cycle(s) of instruction.

Each of these three components is vitally important as you proceed through the various stages and cycles of data-driven decision making.

Although this publication focuses on action planning in the context of a data-driven decision-making framework, it is important to understand that action planning is part of a much more comprehensive process: that of *action research*. Action research is a type of educational research, in that the purpose of educational research is to study various educational phenomena. Simply put, action research *is* educational research. Action research studies can use any type of educational research design with which you might be familiar, including quantitative, qualitative, or mixed-methods. The only real difference between action research and the more traditional forms of educational research has little, if anything, to do with a specific approach, research design, or type of data. Rather, it rests solely in the *underlying purpose for the research*. The main goal of quantitative research is to describe and explain a research problem, whereas the goal of qualitative research is to develop a holistic description of a research situation, often for the purposes of developing theory. The purpose of mixed-methods studies is similar to that of traditional quantitative research: to better understand and explain a research problem. However, the main goal of *action research* is to address local-level problems with the anticipation of finding immediate answers to questions or solutions to problems.

This description ought to sound familiar to you. After all, it is nearly identical to the purpose of data-driven decision making. The reason for this similarity is that the process of data-driven decision making is essentially a foundational concept built into the action research process. Admittedly, the focus of this publication is not to expose the reader to the ins and outs of action research. That said, let's take a brief look at the process of conducting action research to contextualize the concept of action planning.

I view action research as a four-stage cyclical process (Mertler, 2014). Each cycle consists of the following stages:

1. The **planning** stage: planning for your action research.

2. The **acting** stage: implementing your action research.

3. The **developing** stage: developing an action plan for implementation and future cycles of action research.

4. The **reflecting** stage: reflecting on the process.

This process may appear to be linear—or, at least, to include linear components (i.e., first plan, then act, then develop, and finally reflect)—but this is merely to show the relationships that exist between adjacent stages or steps. The process of action research is actually cyclical in nature. Typically, educators design and implement an action research project, collect and analyze data to evaluate its effectiveness, and then make revisions and improvements for future implementation. In all likelihood, the educator would implement the project again—perhaps with next semester's or next year's students—and again monitor its effectiveness and make subsequent revisions. A given project may never have a clear end but goes through continual cycles of implementation, evaluation, and revision from one semester or one year to the next. The outcome, results, or reflections from one cycle of action research provide the impetus for the subsequent cycle.

Again, this should sound familiar: it's very similar to the process for data-driven educational decision making. Just like that process, action research never really ends. The action research may continue along the same line (i.e., topic or problem of interest) in subsequent cycles, or it may branch off in a different direction. This is not unlike an educator's professional growth and development; sometimes, we feel the need to further our professional development in a particular area, whereas other times we think it's important to grow in a different direction.

Why Is Action Planning Important?

Let us focus our attention on the third stage of the action research cycle: the developing stage. In an action research context, the developing stage consists of taking the results from the collection and analysis of data, your interpretations of those results, and the conclusions that you have drawn and decisions made and use all of that information for developing a plan of action for the future (Mertler, 2014). The action plan may consist of strategies for future implementation of interventions or revisions and improvements to instructional practice. You may also include in the action plan ideas and designs for future cycles of action research. Therefore, an action plan is essentially a plan for how the outcomes of a particular action research project will (1) *guide future practice* and (2) *direct future cycles of action research.*

This concept of action planning applies to data-driven decision making in exactly the same manner as it does to an action research framework. Our comprehensive process for data-driven decision making involves the following steps:

1. Identification of a curricular or skill area to target for intervention or instructional revision (based on multiple sources of student data).

2. Development and implementation of the intervention or instructional revision.

3. Ongoing collection and analysis of data resulting from the intervention or instructional revision.

4. Assessment of the effectiveness of the implemented intervention or instructional revision.

5. Development of an action plan for future cycles of intervention or instructional revision.

In this model, action planning becomes a critical factor in the overall effectiveness of interventions or instructional revisions. Failure to reflect on what you have done and to plan appropriately, adequately, and thoughtfully for future cycles will likely result in a lower degree of effectiveness in the long term. The action plan developed in Step 5 *leads directly into and specifically guides* the next stage of problem identification, as well as the development of interventions or instructional revisions. The action plan's quality and attention to detail will ultimately play a huge role in the effectiveness of future cycles of intervention or revision. In addition, professional reflection is a key component in developing these aspects of your action plan.

It is for these reasons that action planning is such a critical step in the process of data-driven decision making. I do not want to imply that action planning is more important than any other step in the process, but it is *at least* as important as every other component and should not be overlooked or considered lightly.

Continuation of Example #2: Action Planning

After addressing the initial problem of student deficiencies in the Data Analysis and Probability strand of the statewide assessment that he had identified from last year's state test results, along with the implemented revisions to his instruction and data that he had collected from this year's students, Mr. Scott had ideas for what he wanted to do next. Although he had developed an informal plan for proceeding with his instructional revisions, he knew that many of the details of what he had done and his ideas for next year might get lost over the summer vacation. Therefore, he believed that it was imperative to record all of this information—including his plan for next year—so that he could refer to it over the summer and next fall.

Mr. Scott recalled that earlier in the school year, his building administrator had shared with the entire faculty a template for developing an action plan. He found the template and sat down during his next planning period to begin developing his own action plan. An excerpt from his plan appears below.

1. *The initial problem I identified was . . .*
   Students were performing poorly on Data Analysis and Probability on the state exam.

2. *The purpose of my intervention/instructional revision was to . . .*

> Resequence and reinforce instruction on this unit so student performance improves.

3. *A summary of my implemented intervention/ instructional revision is . . .*

> Administered a pre-test. Introduced and reinforced concepts from this unit throughout fall term. Required students to keep periodic journals.

4. *Data that I collected and evidence of the effectiveness show that . . .*

> State test results showed improvement on this strand (decrease from 22 percent to 10 percent Below Proficient). Journals supported improved student understanding of these concepts.

5. *Recommendations for changes to my practice for the next cycle of intervention/instructional revision include . . .*

> Reprioritize math strands from results of this year's state test. Identify curricular area/unit to focus attention on for next year. Don't lose sight of this year's improvements!

To give your feedback on this publication and
be entered into a drawing for a free ASCD
Arias e-book, please visit
www.ascd.org/ariasfeedback

ASCD | arias™

ENCORE

DATA-DRIVEN DECISION-MAKING TEMPLATES

This Encore section consists of four templates designed to help teachers through various components of the data-driven decision-making process. The templates provide guiding questions or prompts that facilitate these processes. In addition, I include my own iPad app, which provides templates to guide teachers through a more formal process of classroom-based action research.

5 Why Process for Problem Identification

This template is designed to help you explore cause-and-effect relationships that may underlie a particular classroom problem. The goal is to determine the root cause of the problem, which serves as the most logical starting point for designing interventions or instructional improvements as part of the larger data-driven decision-making process. Each successive "why" question drills deeper into the origins of the problem. Once you believe you have identified the root cause of the original problem, you can end the process. Please note that there is nothing critical in the fact that there are five "whys"; in some situations, you may arrive at the root cause in three "whys" and in others, it may take seven "whys." The particular situation should dictate how long this process goes on.

1. What specific problem have you observed?

2. Why does/doesn't *this* problem (from #1) happen?

3. Why does/doesn't *this* problem (from #2) happen?

4. Why does/doesn't *this* problem (from #3) happen?

5. Why does/doesn't *this* problem (from #4) happen?

6. Why does/doesn't *this* problem (from #5) happen?

Key Questions for Student-Level Decision Making

The following guiding questions are important ones for teachers to consider as they determine the nature, design, and implementation of student-level interventions.

1. The curricular area to be targeted for this student is . . .

2. Individual student data that led me to target this content/skill set included . . .

3. KEY QUESTION: *Where is this content addressed in our district's curriculum?*

4. KEY QUESTION: *At what point in the school year are these concepts/skills taught?*

5. KEY QUESTION: *How are students taught these concepts/skills, and how has this student responded to this format of instruction?*

6. KEY QUESTION: *How has this student been required to demonstrate mastery of these concepts/skills? How has this student responded to this format of assessment?*

Key Questions for Group-Level Decision Making

The following guiding questions are important ones for teachers to consider as they determine the nature, design, and implementation of group-level instructional revisions.

1. The curricular area to be targeted is . . .

2. Data that led me to target this content/skill set included . . .

3. KEY QUESTION: *Where is this content addressed in our district's curriculum?*

4. KEY QUESTION: *At what point in the school year are these concepts/skills taught?*

5. KEY QUESTION: *How are students taught these concepts/skills?*

6. KEY QUESTION: *How are students required to demonstrate mastery of these concepts/skills? In other words, how are they assessed in the classroom?*

Action Planning Template

This template is designed to help you track and maintain records of the initial problem you encountered, the intervention or revised instruction you implemented, the data you collected as evidence of the effectiveness of your efforts, and plans for your next cycle(s) of instruction.

1. *The initial problem I identified was . . .*

2. *The purpose of my intervention/instructional revision was to . . .*

3. *A summary of my implemented intervention/ instructional revision is . . .*

4. *Data that I collected and evidence of the effectiveness show that . . .*

5. *Recommendations for changes to my practice for the next cycle of intervention/instructional revision include . . .*

The Action Research Mentor App for iPad

The *Action Research Mentor* (available at https:// itunes.apple.com/us/app/action-research-mentor/ id778749900?mt=8) is an app I developed consisting of a series of templates designed to guide teachers who are interested in pursuing more formal action research studies. The *Action Research Mentor* assists professional educators in designing action research studies for their particular settings. Teachers must make many important methodological decisions when designing and conducting action research studies. If these decisions are not made carefully and thoughtfully, there may be unexpected negative ramifications later in the study. What educators need is guidance to help them make sound decisions before, during, and after their administration of the action research study.

The *Action Research Mentor* provides focused questions and prompts that guide the user in making these decisions throughout the four stages of the action research process, including the planning stage, the acting stage, the developing stage, and reflecting stage. The app provides direction and mentorship during each stage of the action research process:

1. *The Planning Stage*
   - 5 Why Process for Problem Identification
   - Organizing Your Literature Review
   - Developing a Research Plan

2. *The Acting Stage*
   - Planning for Data Collection
   - Planning for Data Analysis

3. *The Developing Stage*
   - Action Planning

4. *The Reflecting Stage*
- Reflecting on the Action Research Process

Once the user has answered the questions and addressed each prompt, "pages" can be printed or e-mailed (for example, to a professor, an advisor, a supervisor, or an administrator).

References

Chase, C. I. (1999). *Contemporary assessment for educators*. Boston: Allyn and Bacon.

LaFee, S. (2002). Data-driven districts. *School Administrator, 59*(11), 6–7, 9–10, 12, 14–15.

Mertler, C. A. (2002). *Using standardized test data to guide instruction and intervention*. (ERIC Document Reproduction Service No. ED 470589). Available: http://files.eric.ed.gov/fulltext/ED470589.pdf

Mertler, C. A. (2003). *Classroom assessment: A practical guide for educators*. Los Angeles: Pyrczak.

Mertler, C. A. (2007). *Interpreting standardized test scores: Strategies for data-driven instructional decision making*. Los Angeles: Sage.

Mertler, C. A. (2009). A systematic approach to transforming the art of teaching into the science of teaching: Developing a D-DIDM mind-set (MWERA 2008 Presidential Address). *Mid-Western Educational Researcher, 22*(1), 12–23.

Mertler, C. A. (2014). *Action research: Improving schools and empowering educators* (4th ed.). Los Angeles: Sage.

Mertler, C. A., & Zachel, K. (2006). Data-driven instructional decision making: An idea (and practice) whose time has come. *Principal Navigator, 1*(3), 6–9.

Russell, M. K., & Airasian, P. W. (2012). *Classroom assessment: Concepts and applications* (7th ed.). Boston: McGraw-Hill.

Related Resources

At the time of publication, the following ASCD resources were available (ASCD stock numbers appear in parentheses). For up-to-date information about ASCD resources, go to www.ascd.org. You can search the complete archives of Educational Leadership at http://www.ascd.org/el.

ASCD EDge©
Exchange ideas and connect with other educators interested in various topics, including Action Research and PLCs, on the social networking site ASCD EDge at http://ascdedge.ascd.org.

Print Products
The Art and Science of Teaching: A Comprehensive Framework for Effective Instruction by Robert J. Marzano (#107001)

How Teachers Can Turn Data into Action by Daniel R. Venables (#114007)

Improving Teaching with Collaborative Action Research: An ASCD Action Tool by Diane Cunningham (#111006)

Using Data to Focus Instructional Improvement by Diane K. Lapp, Nancy E. Frey, Douglas B. Fisher, and Cheryl James-Ward (#113003)

ASCD PD Online© Courses
Using Data to Determine Student Mastery (#PD14OC001)

This and other online courses are available at www.ascd.org/pdonline.

DVDs
Examining Student Work (#601283)

Using Classroom Assessment to Guide Instruction (#602286)

A Visit to a Data-Driven School District (#606059)

For more information: send e-mail to member@ascd.org; call 1-800-933-2723 or 703-578-9600, press 2; send a fax to 703-575-5400; or write to Information Services, ASCD, 1703 N. Beauregard St., Alexandria, VA 22311-1714 USA.

About the Author

Craig A. Mertler has been an educator for 29 years—18 of those in higher education and 6 as an administrator—having begun his career as a high school science teacher. He has taught courses focused on the application of action research to promote educator empowerment, school improvement, and job-embedded professional development, and also teaches research methods, statistical analyses, and educational assessment methods. He has served as the research methodology expert on more than 100 doctoral dissertations and Masters theses. He is the author of 20 books, four invited book chapters, and 18 refereed journal articles. He has presented more than 35 research papers at professional meetings. He has consulted with numerous schools and districts on the broad topic of classroom assessment, data-driven decision making, and classroom-based action research. He currently operates an educational consulting firm and can be reached at craig.mertler@gmail.com. More about Dr. Mertler and his areas of consulting expertise can be found at www.craigmertler.com/mec.

WHAT KEEPS YOU UP AT NIGHT?

ASCD Arias begin with a burning question and then provide the answers you need today—in a convenient format you can read in one sitting and immediately put into practice. Available in both print and digital editions.

Answers You Need
from Voices You Trust

ASCD | arias™